Seasons

Summer

Siân Smith

Heinemann Library
Chicago, Illinois

Editorial: Rebecca Rissman, Charlotte Guillain, and Siân Smith
Picture research: Elizabeth Alexander and Sally Claxton
Designed by Joanna Hinton-Malivoire
Printed and bound by South China Printing Company Limited

13 12 11 10
10 9 8 7 6 5 4 3

ISBN-13: 978-1-4329-2729-5 (hc)
ISBN-13: 978-1-4329-2734-9 (pb)

Library of Congress Cataloging-in-Publication Data
Smith, Siân.
  Summer / Siân Smith.
      p. cm. -- (Seasons)
  Includes bibliographical references and index.
  1. Summer--Juvenile literature. I. Title.
  QB637.6.S65 2008
  508.2--dc22
                                2008049157
Acknowledgments
The author and publisher are grateful to the following for permission to reproduce copyright material:
©Alamy pp.**15** (Alex Segre), **19** (Arco Images GmbH), **14** (Blend Images), **13** (Bubbles Photolibrary), **18** (Image Source Black), **21** (Imagestate), **20** (Jon Arnold Images Ltd.), **12** (Jupiter Images/Thinkstock), **8** (Nick Baylis), **11, 23 bottom** (Romain Bayle), **9** (Simone van den Berg); ©Capstone Global Library Ltd. p.**16** (2005/Malcolm Harris); ©Corbis pp.**04 br** (Image100), **04 tl** (Zefa/Roman Flury); ©Digital Vision p.**17** (Rob van Petten); ©Getty Images pp.**10** (Ariel Skelley), **04 tr** (Floria Werner), **7** (IIC/ Axiom), **5** (Kazuo Ogawa/Sebun Photo); ©iStockphoto pp.**6, 23 top** (Bojan Tezak), **04 bl** (Inga Ivanova), **22** (Tatiana Grozetskaya).
Cover photograph of a meadow reproduced with permission of ©Shutterstock (Katerina Havelkova). Back cover photograph reproduced with permission of ©Digital Vision (Rob Van Patten).

Every effort has been made to contact copyright holders of any material reproduced in this book. Any omissions will be rectified in subsequent printings if notice is given to the publisher.

Contents

What Is Summer?

spring

summer

fall

winter

There are four seasons every year.

4

Summer is one of the four seasons.

When Is Summer?

spring

summer

winter

fall

The four seasons follow a pattern

Summer comes after spring.

The Weather in Summer

It can be sunny in summer.

It can be hot in summer.

What Can We See in Summer?

In summer we can see people wearing t-shirts.

In summer we can see people wearing sandals.

In summer we can see people wearing hats.

In summer we can see people
wearing sunscreen.

In summer we can see people
gardening.

In summer we can see people
swimming.

In summer we can see people going to the beach.

In summer we can see people going
to the park.

In summer we can see ice cream.

In summer we can see fruit.

In summer we can see flowers.

20

In summer we can see bees.

Which Season Comes Next?

Which season comes after summer?

Picture Glossary

pattern happening in the same order

sandal type of shoe with an open top

Index

Note to Parents and Teachers
Before reading
Talk to the children about the four seasons of the year: spring, summer, fall, winter. Ask the children when their birthdays are and tell them which season their birthday falls in.
Talk to the children about the different things they do in summer. What sort of clothes do they wear? Do they eat any different foods? Do they like the summer better than any of the other seasons?

After reading
Make summer flowers. You will need colored paper, scissors, pencils/crayons, straws, and tape. Tell the children to choose a sheet of paper of any color they like for their flower. Tell them to trace around their hand as many times as possible on the paper. Then, help children cut out the hands. Pinch all the bases of the "hands" together and tape them onto the straw. Separate out the petals (fingers) by pulling gently away from the center. Help children cut leaves out of green paper and attach them to the stem (straw).

Memory game. Place pictures of items associated with summer on a tray. For example: a sun, sandcastle, strawberries, sunglasses, and a sun hat. Tell the children to look at the objects for 20 seconds. Then turn away from the children and remove one of the pictures. Turn back and ask the children what is missing.